Praise for *Ingredients of Empathy*

"A book to be devoured! *Ingredients of Empathy* offers thoughtful, practical insights on cultivating empathy in both our personal and professional lives, showing how small acts of care can make such a profound impact. These lessons are beautifully interwoven with delicious recipes that nourish both body and spirit."

– Miguel Ávila, Editor-in-Chief, *The Portuguese Tribune* | *Tribuna Portuguesa*, San José, California

"Ana and Pam's book offers something we really need today — a clear and engaging guide to rediscovering our empathy. Their real-life examples are relatable and practical, and the warm, accessible writing style makes this a book I'll return to again and again."

– Erin Rand, COO and Serial Business Scaler

"*Ingredients of Empathy* masterfully tackles all the basics and specifics of empathy. This readable little book has the potential to make a meaningful difference in the lives of anyone who reads it. It combines clear explanations with practical tips on how to be a person who recognizes and respects the innate dignity of others. Oh, if everyone would practice what Pam and Ana preach, the world would be a much happier place. Including recipes after each chapter was sheer genius. What better way to connect than through a shared table!"

– Michelle Helvey, Head of School

"As life moves ever faster and technology continues to disconnect us, there has never been a more important time to be reminded of the impact of showing empathy and the healing power of receiving it ourselves."

– Tammy Estes, Former Chief Product Officer, Nomadix

"Pam and Ana have found the key ingredient to heal healthcare and the world — breaking bread together at a table unleashes empathy that lifts up humanity. A must read to heal the world."

– Bridget Duffy, Raving Fan and First Chief Experience Officer in Healthcare in the US

"*Ingredients of Empathy* is an unexpectedly creative way to talk about empathy. It's a super easy read that mixes solid expert advice with relatable personal stories and — believe it or not — recipes! I loved the cooking metaphors, like leaving the ingredients of "comparison and criticism" out when serving up empathy. It's a great reminder that empathy belongs in everyday moments, not just during a crisis. It's a down-to-earth guide on how to show up for people."

– Colleen Blake, COO, People Leader, and Mother of Three

"Truly a "Recipe for a Better World!" While I like to consider myself an empathetic person, *Ingredients of Empathy* reminded me of the basics and the assembled ingredients in a way that helps me better understand and implement them in my own life, so I can also impact the lives of those around me. I want to share it with everyone around me, primarily through modeling in my own life!"

– Ted Helvey, Managing Partner, Gate Worldwide Holdings

"In today's world, we need more empathy to make it a better place, and being an empath myself, I also learned something new. People don't realize how strong a word (or action) can make an outcome positive or negative. *Ingredients of Empathy* gives beautiful, clear, and uncomplicated examples of how to show empathy to those who need it and to those in just everyday conversation. I love all the recipes after each chapter, which is a nice bonus other books don't have!"

– Debbie Kitani, Friend

"What a heartfelt combination — two friends, Pam and Ana succinctly weave warmth and thoughtful life lessons with family, neighbors, the workplace, and strangers, recognizing our roles and the effect we have impacting others in a positive way. Chapters pair theory with hands-on experience — through storytelling, you see the power of listening and how it heals wounds. Read *Ingredients of Empathy*! Become a better person."

– Robert Haefling, CEO & Chairman Icron Technologies (Retired)

Ingredients of Empathy

A Recipe for a Better World

Ana Lúcia Correia and Pamela Kay Gonçalves

Published by How2Conquer
Atlanta, Georgia
www.how2conquer.com

How2Conquer is an imprint of White Deer Publishing, LLC.
www.whitedeerpublishing.net

First edition, April 2026
Ebook edition created 2026

Illustrations and cover design by Telia Garner
Edited by Lauren Kelliher and Charlotte Bleau

Library of Congress Cataloging-in-Publication Data is on file at the Library of Congress, Washington, DC.

Print ISBN 978-1-945783-54-8
Ebook ISBN 978-1-945783-55-5

For information about special discounts available for bulk purchases, please contact How2Conquer Special Sales at www.how2conquer.com/bulk-orders.

Ana dedicates this book to her parents, Aníbal and Maria de Fátima, her grandmother, Luísa, her children, Tatiana and Eduardo, and her grandchildren, Salvador, Vicente, and Mateus.

Pam dedicates this book to her husband, António and their children, Gary, Tatiana, and Katya, and their granddaughter, Sofia.

Contents

Introduction 1
Section 1: What Is Empathy? 5
Key Ingredients of Empathy 7
Everyone Is a Pedestrian 13
Section 2: Why, When, and Where Is Empathy Needed? 19
Bringing Light to a Dark World 21
Making Time for Empathy 25
Empathy in the Workplace 29
Section 3: Roadblocks to Empathy 37
Comparison and Criticism 39
Empathy Fatigue 43
Section 4: Expressing Empathy 49
Empathy's Native Tongue 51
Section 5: Building, Sharing, and Receiving Empathy 65
The Data Behind Empathy 67
Sharing Our Stories 71
Receiving Empathy 75
Wrap Up & Quick Tips 81
Paying It Forward 83
Resources 87
Recipe Index 91

Acknowledgments 93
About the Authors 95
Recipes 97
Starters 98
Mains 102
Desserts 109

Introduction

We had been friends for several years already, but our jobs made it difficult to get together. Ana was a chef at a busy, local restaurant in Portugal, and Pam, having moved to a village close by with her husband nine years prior, still worked in marketing for a U.S. company with staggered time zones, so we could only grab a few moments here and there to catch up.

On November 11, 2023, a Saturday for Pam, and a day off for Ana with the restaurant closed for staff vacation, we were able to enjoy a leisurely lunch, talk about our lives, and contemplate how we could solve the world's problems, if given the chance. Suddenly Ana looked up and said, "We should write a book about empathy." From that one comment, the seed of inspiration was planted, and we quickly agreed that we would set out to do just that.

While Ana gets full credit for coming up with this idea, we co-authored *Ingredients of Empathy* to remind us that we can't get through life on our own.

Our approach was to use universal examples that hopefully extend to several cultures. We looked at best practices from different parts of the world, learning about how various societies express empathy in little ways every day. No matter how familiar or far away, these expressions are simple, common-sense approaches that can be adopted into our own lives. The goal was to connect human to human, using laypersons' words. Given Ana's ability in the kitchen and that bringing someone a meal is a universally recognized show of empathy, we decided to include some of our favorite recipes for you to share with anyone you'd like to extend a little empathy to.

We hope our readers find inspirational ideas on sharing empathy and will also try some new dishes to share.

Happy reading and cooking,

Ana and Pam

EMPATHY

Section 1:
What Is Empathy?

We all have a rough idea of what empathy is, but we often confuse it with sympathy. Starting with the wrong definition can lead to the wrong behavior, however unintentional, and damage our connections with others. At the same time, we often think empathy is something reserved for everyone else, but all of us need empathy at some point in our lives. These first two chapters will set us on the right path.

Key Ingredients of Empathy

"Empathy is the greatest virtue. From it, all virtues flow. Without it, all virtues are an act." – Eric Zorn, Author

We don't recall learning about a specific virtue called empathy. In school or church, we might have studied about temperance, wisdom, justice, or courage . . . but calling empathy the greatest virtue, as Eric Zorn does, is a tall order. As we dove into this important topic, we realized that empathy draws from other parts of our character, these other virtues. Empathy is the ultimate, outward emotion that delivers a bundle of virtues to benefit other people.

So, if it's a virtue, how do we develop empathy? Let's first talk about what empathy is — and what it's not. In our research, we found that many people think that empathy and sympathy are synonymous. One of our favorite authors is Dr. Brené Brown, a researcher who helps people like us understand complex topics in a down-to-earth, relatable fashion. When Dr. Brown presents, she helps put into words what most of us are feeling and does it with grace, humility, and humor. In a short video called *Brené Brown on Empathy*, she tells us that empathy fuels connection, while sympathy drives disconnection. The disconnection happens because sympathy includes some judgment of the other person. This judgment can happen in our minds or aloud, but generally sounds like "How did you get yourself in this situation?" or, "Sounds like some of this is your fault." The disconnection continues when we try to "help," often offering free advice about how to improve the situation without really acknowledging their feelings. Or we speak in platitudes without sharing in their pain: "Sorry for your loss" or, "At least you still have a job."

But empathy just looks different. The emotion the other person is feeling is reflected back from our own words and expressions. We're not judging; we're in the foxhole together, making a connection. Empathy means we're taking the other person's experience as they have described it and not trying to make it conform or compare to our own experiences or biases.

The work of nursing scholar Dr. Teresa Wiseman elaborates on the difference and offers practicable approaches to connecting with empathy instead of distancing ourselves with sympathy. From her research, we learn that there are four key ingredients of empathy:

1. **Taking on someone else's perspective**
   When we take on the perspective of another person, we must also be able to recognize someone else's perspective as truth.
2. **Being non-judgmental**
   When we judge another person's situation, we discount their experience. To take on the perspective of another person, we must set aside our own thoughts, assumptions, and biases.
3. **Recognizing someone else's emotions or understanding their feelings**
   Recognizing and understanding someone else's emotions requires us to be in touch with our own feelings and to put ourselves aside so we can focus on the person in distress.
4. **Communicating your understanding of a person's feelings**
   We have to express our understanding of someone's emotions or feelings and also validate them. Validating someone's feelings demonstrates that we accept, acknowledge, and understand them.

One story we've captured from a young Portuguese woman who overheard a conversation between her aunts went something like this:

> "During the surgery, I saw a bright light at the end of a tunnel," one aunt said.
> "Oh, I was so sick the other day, I saw two bright lights," the other aunt said.

For some reason, when people put their emotions and experiences out there, it often sparks a strange competitive streak in us to prove that regardless of what's going on with them, our situation is somehow worse. This is NOT empathy. Also, we're not sure what that aunt was seeing, but it sounded like those could have been the headlights of an oncoming car.

Pam's mother-in-law often complained about her health. She told Pam, "If I don't talk about it, people won't know that I'm really sick and will think that everything is normal." What a sad statement, but we can see some truth in it. One of the secret ingredients of empathy is to listen more than we talk. If you look at Dr. Wiseman's four points, three of them require very little speaking, if any at all. So, let's break this down into an everyday example.

A woman arrives home after a long day at work, which requires being on her feet for most of her shift. She's greeted at the door by two children who demand her immediate attention. She sees her husband sitting on the couch, from where he says, "Hi, honey," and half-heartedly calls out to the kids to leave Mom alone.

A more empathetic response from the husband could be to greet his wife at the door himself, giving her a hug that communicates "I'm glad you're home." Never underestimate the power of a good hug. A good hug can raise our levels of oxytocin, relieving stress and releasing dopamine and serotonin that improve our mood. The husband could take one more step to tell his wife, "I know you've been on your feet all day. Why don't you put your feet up while the kids and I finish dinner?"

Of course, this works in reverse with any close partner, but this example checks off several ingredients of empathy. The husband puts himself figuratively in his wife's shoes, taking on her perspective, recognizing her physical state, communicating an overall understanding of her situation and feelings. He also doesn't jump in with his own thoughts and judgments, which is key. It's not a contest about who is the most tired; it's validating the other person's feelings, period. He's also providing a model of empathy to their children.

Let's imagine a world in which these everyday interactions are done with empathy. How much stronger and kinder our relationships would be — at home, in school, at work, in church, and in our community!

Food for Thought

1 Empathy is a key virtue but is not the same as sympathy, which implies judgment and causes disconnection. Empathy requires understanding and drives a connection.

2 The key ingredients of empathy are:

- Taking on someone else's perspective.
- Being non-judgmental.
- Recognizing someone else's feelings.
- Communicating your understanding of those feelings.

3 Practice empathy today on someone close to you.

A Recipe to Share

Here's a recipe for someone who's been on their feet all day — and "plating" the dish adds that special touch to the experience.

Ingredients

- 1 ½ cups linguini
- 3 tbsp olive oil
- ¼ cup margarine
- 3 cloves garlic, crushed
- 1 bay leaf
- 1 small chili pepper, broken in half
- 1 tsp sweet pepper powder
- 20 shrimp, peeled and deveined
- Salt and pepper
- 1 tbsp brandy
- 1 tbsp white wine
- 10 cherry tomatoes, leave whole
- Grated Parmesan cheese
- Chopped parsley

Preparation

1. Cook the linguini in salted water to package instructions. Ana prefers to cook this "al dente."
2. Sauté garlic in a wok with olive oil and margarine.
3. Add the bay leaf, chili pepper, and sweet pepper powder.

4. Once the garlic browns, add the shrimp. Season with salt and pepper.
5. Drain the linguini, saving some of the water.
6. Continue to sauté the shrimp mixture and add the brandy and white wine. Let it flame a little and add the cherry tomatoes to the middle of the pan.
7. Add the linguini to the shrimp with a little of the linguini cooking water. Sauté for 2 to 3 minutes to absorb the flavor of the shrimp.
8. Remove from the heat and plate the dish to your liking.
9. Serve with Parmesan cheese and chopped parsley.

Everyone Is a Pedestrian

"Learning to stand in someone else's shoes, to see through their eyes, that's how peace begins. And it's up to you to make that happen. Empathy is a quality of character that can change the world." – Barack Obama, 44th President of the United States

We've all experienced erratic drivers in a parking lot. As pedestrians, we're a little wary of crossing their paths. But isn't it strange that some drivers care so little about pedestrians, when after they park their cars, they indeed become pedestrians themselves?

It's easy to ignore someone else's plight, to be dismissive, judgmental, or even to ridicule another's situation. But we should all remember that, at some point in our lives, probably oftentimes, we are all pedestrians who need empathy.

We're human, and sometimes irrational thoughts cloud our common sense. How many times have we begrudgingly passed an empty handicapped parking space, somehow thinking only of our own needs ("I could really use that parking space."), and not realizing how difficult it must be for those requiring wheelchairs after parking?

The intent of these examples is not to make us feel shame, rather, it's to simply put ourselves in someone else's reality, someone else's path, and create connections with others that say, "I understand and empathize what you're going through."

One of the most important things we teach our children once they're walking and out of their strollers is how to cross a street safely. We teach them the rules: use the crosswalk, look both ways before crossing, make sure drivers can see you. We offer examples (good or bad) to our children when we drive.

Wouldn't it be wonderful if we taught empathy in the same way to our children, starting when they are young, providing real-life examples as they grow, and continuing to train them on how to show empathy as young adults?

There are studies that show teaching empathy to school children can lower the rate of bullying and feelings of isolation, as well as improve grades. We go into more depth about **The Data Behind Empathy** in Section 5, but the research shows that with empathy, the world really can be a better place.

Contrary to what many people think, empathy is not just a feeling; it's also a behavior. As we mentioned in the last chapter, a key ingredient of empathy is listening. As the saying goes, we have two ears and one mouth, so we're probably meant to listen at least twice as much as we speak. Unfortunately, human nature errs on the side of judging without knowing, giving advice without listening, or not even wanting to understand the motives, reasons, or feelings that led that person to their current condition.

Let's consider the teachings of Carl Rogers, an American psychologist known especially for his person-centered psychotherapy. He wrote about three core principles he used in counseling:

1. **Unconditional positive regard** — non-judgmental and non-problem-solving listening.
2. **Empathic listening** — showing genuine care.
3. **Client-centered approach** — focus on the other, not on the self.

We tend to go into problem-solving mode or quietly judge when others begin to share their situations. Keeping these habits at bay is difficult, but it's something we must do to be truly empathetic. Showing genuine care through our body language (nodding in comprehension as the other person is talking and periodic verbal acknowledgments, for example), demonstrates that we're actively listening and supporting. What Dr. Rogers meant by a client-centered approach is something we raised in the previous chapter. Our focus should be on the other person; this is not the time to bring our own problems into the conversation. That diminishes the importance of the other person's plight.

Consider this passage written by Margaret Wheatley from an article she wrote called "Listening as Healing:"

> *"Listening is such a simple act. It requires us to be present, and that takes practice, but we don't have to do anything else. We don't have to advise, or coach, or sound wise. We just have to be willing to sit there and listen. If we can do that, we create moments in which real healing is available. Whatever life we have experienced, if we can tell our story to someone who listens, we find it easier to deal with our circumstances."*

We feel less vulnerable when we're driving our cars and can get from point A to point B fairly easily. But life happens — sometimes cars break down, and we're waiting for a good Samaritan to stop and help push us to safety. And while we're waiting, we become pedestrians. We might even get angry stares and judgmental looks from other drivers and passengers. Don't we realize that helping another get unstuck will make traffic flow more easily for everyone on the road? Consider stopping, listening, and helping others get to an emotionally safe place, with empathy and grace.

Food for Thought

1	We're all in need of empathy at some point in our lives.
2	We should begin teaching empathy early in life.
3	Showing empathy means listening and caring without judging or problem-solving.
4	Think of someone who needs an empathetic ear.

A Recipe to Share

One of the pedestrians we might see in our little town is Ana, who shops daily at the local markets. But once in the kitchen, she's known as Lucy, an anglicized version of Lúcia, her middle name. Here is her special fish recipe. You can accompany it with boiled potatoes, mashed potatoes, or rice.

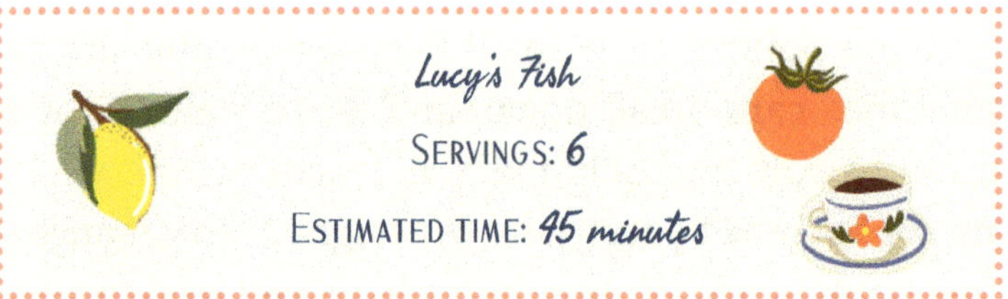

Ingredients

- Olive oil
- 4 medium onions, cut in wedges
- 2 garlic cloves, chopped
- 1 chili pepper, whole
- ½ red bell pepper, cut in rounds

- ½ green bell pepper, cut in rounds
- 8 oz canned peeled tomatoes
- 1 bay leaf
- White wine
- 6 pieces of white fish (croaker recommended, or sea bass)
- 1 oz whiskey
- Soy sauce
- Oregano
- Parsley, chopped

Preparation

1. In a pan, add a drizzle of olive oil and the onion. Heat on high until lightly browned.
2. Add the garlic, chili pepper, and bell peppers.
3. After letting it brown a little, add the peeled tomatoes, bay leaf, and white wine. Lower the heat and simmer for 15 minutes.
4. Salt the fish, add it to the pan, and cook for 10 minutes.
5. Check if the fish is cooked (if flaky with a fork) and add whiskey, soy sauce, and oregano to taste.
6. Adjust the seasoning, garnish with parsley, and it's ready to serve.

Section 2:

Why, When, and Where Is Empathy Needed?

We all share in the human experience. For some of us, life can be pretty tough, and we need to connect with others to keep us from falling into despair. We can bring light and hope to others in both everyday gestures and life-changing actions. Once we decide to find and create time to share empathy in the twenty-four hours we're given each day, we must decide when, where, and how to take opportunities to practice.

Bringing Light to a Dark World

"Light is to darkness what love is to fear; in the presence of one the other disappears." – Marianne Williamson, Author

Some people believe that if we wake up in the morning, then there must be a reason why we're still alive, that there's something worthwhile to accomplish on this day. But for many, getting out of bed some days just seems impossible, and instead of embracing what's ahead, they feel dread or anxiety. For these and others, how can we bring light to their darkness?

One of our favorite authors is Corrie ten Boom, a survivor of the Holocaust and author of *The Hiding Place*. One quote from *The Hiding Place* says, "There is no pit so deep, that God's love is not deeper still." One way we can show light is through our faith, which helps us rise above our circumstances. This faith demonstrates that there is hope, and as believers in the power of prayer, we know that God can make a miracle out of a mess.

We know that not everyone shares the same faith, but we all share our humanity and the power to perform acts of kindness to bring brightness into the lives of others. These can range from everyday gestures: telling someone thank you, offering a smile, greeting a passerby, looking a waitress in the eye while ordering, or letting a busy mom cut in front of you at the grocery store. The best part of humanity is reminding people that they belong to the human race and that they matter, regardless of their circumstances.

Other larger initiatives might bring the life-changing light that keeps another from deep despair. Let's consider the role of a lighthouse. During the day, it's on the lookout for ships in distress. At night, it's the reference point toward a safe shore. Without even being aware, we may be someone else's lighthouse. If we find ourselves often surrounded by others in pain and distress, seeking comfort and safety, we become human lighthouses, and that comes with a certain level of responsibility.

We should be careful not to judge someone coming to us for help. Lighthouses don't discriminate against shipping vessels because of their size, paint color, speed, or country of origin. Nor do they judge a ship's choices or circumstances that brought them to seek refuge in the first place. They simply exist as a guide, a beacon, and a safe haven. As human lighthouses, let's put aside our prejudices and biases to help our fellow humans.

Larger "lighthouse" initiatives take resources (time, treasure, or talent). Cooking for someone who's ill or a busy caregiver (the impetus for including recipes), spending time with the elderly, donating time, blood, or money to a nonprofit are all practical ways to bring light to a dark situation. One word of caution: we can't neglect our own needs while helping others, which can lead to burnout. Even lighthouses need to keep their own lights in good working order to remain effective.

Let's also dismiss the notion that people should "go it alone" or "pick themselves up by their bootstraps." We're not designed to live alone or to be isolated. Humans need other humans. And while it's easy to believe that empathy should start with others, or those in power or the famous or wealthy, our empathy can begin with us and one other person at a time.

From the same article referenced in **Everyone Is a Pedestrian** in Section 1, Margaret Wheatley writes, "Our natural state is to be together. Though we keep moving away from each other, we haven't lost the need to be in relationship. Everybody has a story, and everybody wants to tell their story in order to connect. If no one listens, we tell it to ourselves and then we go mad."

Bringing light to one another makes us connect as humans and offers another key ingredient of empathy.

Food for Thought

1	We can share light with humanity through everyday acts of kindness.
2	Sometimes we can be a human lighthouse for others, to keep them from despair.
3	We also need to take care of ourselves, so we don't neglect our own needs.
4	We all have a story to share, and that's what keeps us connected as humans.

A Recipe to Share

The lighthouse in Cabo da Roca, Portugal, is the westernmost part of continental Europe and an hour's drive from where we live. After a tour of the area, it's good to be able to come home and whip up an easy snack, like the recipe below, which is also a typical starter in many Portuguese restaurants.

---

1 Farinheira is a Portuguese smoked sausage made with wheat flour and pork fat.

Ingredients

- Olive oil
- ½ ripe tomato, diced
- ½ Farinheira sausage (or pork sausage if unavailable)
- 1 chili pepper, sliced in rounds
- 3 eggs
- Salt
- Parsley

Preparation

1. Cut the farinheira in half and remove the skin.
2. Add a little olive oil to a pan and bring to a heat.
3. Add the tomatoes and farinheira and let everything braise.
4. Beat the eggs with a fork and add to the mixture.
5. Stir until eggs are cooked and remove from the heat.
6. Chop some parsley and place on top of the eggs.
7. It's ready to serve.

Making Time for Empathy

"Empathy takes time, and efficiency is for things, not for people." – Stephen Covey, Educator and Author

Time is an interesting dimension. We're all given the same finite amount of time each day, and while we may think we have no choice in how we spend it, that's not completely true. For adults who live in freedom, our days and nights are filled with what we've allowed to enter into our lives and with the consequences of our choices and decisions. The twenty-first-century phenomenon of "I don't have time to sleep, eat, do errands, study, exercise, etc." is usually a self-inflicted wound. Just consider when an unexpected event happens in our lives: the death of a loved one, a sick child, or a car accident. Suddenly, our priorities change, and we do, in fact, make time for other activities.

Empathy may come naturally to some of us. For others, it's a new habit we need to develop. But as with anything else, we need to set aside time to make empathy a priority and to practice our empathy skills. Our readers are probably wondering how we can predict when someone will need our empathy. The truth is, we can't, but we're suggesting building in some extra time to share empathy around us. Here's what that might look like.

We all have friends who, through circumstances or choice, find themselves lonely, depressed, anxious, or frightened. Trying to have a quick phone call or exchanging superficial messages on social media doesn't lend ourselves to sharing empathy. Our suggestion for these friends is to set aside some dedicated time to allow for deeper conversations and above all, listening. This could be through a longer phone call without distractions around us or meeting up in person for a coffee or meal.

Pam's neighbor is an eighty-year-old widow whose grown children live far away. Because of some health problems, it's difficult for Dona Palmira to be away from her home for long periods of time. Thankfully, there's a good network of neighbors who help her with grocery shopping and gardening. But Pam's way of showing empathy is to set aside some time on Sundays to visit Dona Palmira in her home for a coffee, where they can spend time chatting.

There are a couple of memorable moments that happen during these coffee chats. First, Dona Palmira makes coffee with a special cake or biscuits, giving her a chance to host in her own home, and offers a way for her to give back. Plus, she has time to chat with another person about current events, her children and grandchildren, as well as her past. This is all about connecting, human to human, even if our lives are different from those around us. The key ingredient to all of this is scheduling a set time to have these visits, without looking at the clock, without thinking about all the chores and errands we have yet to do, and just listening more than we talk.

There's a quote attributed to Mother Teresa that says, "If you judge people, you have no time to love them." Our very human nature might turn into both judge and jury when we think about the people from the examples we've provided. It's simple in our minds to think, "Why doesn't the depressed person seek clinical help?" or, "Why doesn't the widow move closer to her family?"

But our role is not to judge someone else's actions or character. Empathy is meeting the other person where they are on life's journey and saying, "I'm here for you. I'm sorry this is happening."

Humans are the only species that can anticipate the future. Some look to the future with hope, others with despair, while still others prefer not to think about it at all. When we set aside dedicated time for empathy, the person on the receiving end looks forward to our calls and conversations and feels a sense of hope.

Food for Thought

1	We need to make time for empathy, for longer conversations and listening.
2	Our role is not to judge; it's to meet another where they are on their journey.
3	We can provide hope to others by setting aside dedicated time for empathy.
4	How can we build time for empathy into our busy schedules?

A Recipe to Share

Codfish bears the nickname "Faithful Friend" in Portugal because it's featured at every important meal and stays well preserved when salted and dried. There are hundreds of ways to make cod, but below is one of Portugal's most popular, named after its inventor, José Luís Gomes de Sá Júnior, a cod merchant from Porto.

Ingredients

- 2 cod fillets
- 4 large potatoes, halved, skin on
- 1 ½ tbsp olive oil
- 2 large onions, cut in rounds
- 1 clove garlic, minced
- 8 oz cooked garbanzo beans
- Salt and pepper
- 4 eggs, boiled and sliced in rounds
- Black olives
- 1 sprig parsley

Preparation

1. Preheat oven to 390°F
2. Boil water in a pan and add the cod. Boil for 7 minutes.
3. Remove from the water and remove the skin and bones, then shred.
4. Boil water in a separate pot and salt. Boil potatoes for 10 to 20 minutes, until fork tender.
5. Drain the water and let the potatoes cool slightly. Remove the skin and cut into rounds.
6. Sauté onions and garlic with olive oil in a pan until lightly browned.
7. In a baking dish, add the cod pieces, garbanzo beans, potato rounds, salt, and pepper. Mix carefully so as not to break in pieces or become mushy.
8. Bake for 15 minutes.
9. Remove from the oven and top with boiled eggs, olives, and chopped parsley.
10. Serve the Cod á Gomes de Sá immediately.

Empathy in the Workplace

"Without empathy it is not possible to get the best from your team, so for this reason it is the key to everything." – Satya Nadella, CEO of Microsoft

We spend a good chunk of our lives working — whether in a professional capacity, as a volunteer, or as stay-at-home care providers of the young, elderly, or disabled. So, talking about empathy in the workplace seems like an important and worthwhile topic. One of the real struggles in providing empathy in this setting is to get through to our authentic selves since, at work, we tend to push down our problems and put on a brave face for others. A lot of this comes from genuine fear that we'll be seen as "unprofessional" or "inferior" somehow by our coworkers and management. In the case of volunteers and providers, we might not want to focus on our own issues since the problems of others take priority in our lives.

But several studies point to the benefits of empathy in the workplace. For example, a 2023 EY study of more than 1,000 employed US workers found that companies who had empathy saw an increase in efficiency, revenues, innovation, and job satisfaction. On the other side of the coin, a recent article in Forbes discusses how the findings of Businessolver's 2025 *State of Workplace Empathy Report* "links $180 billion in annual attrition costs to the gap between how empathetic leaders think they are and how supported employees actually feel." The article goes on to say that the report found "over half of employees would take a pay cut to work somewhere more empathetic."

According to Simon Sinek, "Empathy is the foundation of collaboration and innovation." He says, "when you lead with empathy, you make your subordinates feel safe." Sinek attributes this to the release of oxytocin (something we discussed in **Key Ingredients of Empathy** in Section 1) — "the neurochemical that controls feelings of trust, belonging, and happiness."

Reflecting on our own work experiences, we can mostly agree that we perform better in a work environment in which others care about us as people, support our individual needs, show patience with us in our weak areas, and genuinely want us to be successful. The research says that employees will take more risks, be more creative, and experience higher job satisfaction with more empathy in the workplace.

Any given workforce will have employees at different stages of their careers. Some are novices, some are close to retirement, and there are a whole lot of people in between. At each stage, there are various life events to juggle. For example, Pam remembers a time when one of her coworkers complained about a young mother who took off time to nurse a sick child or left early to catch a school play or a game. Pam gently reminded her colleague about the times others picked up the load when their children were young (albeit at different companies back then) and that it was now their time to look out for the next generation. Perspectives were changed, and the team became more empathetic.

We know not everyone shows up in their best form every day. We need to be able to offer grace when needed. As parents we know, for example, that we can have everything ready to go — the kids are dressed, we've got our coffee and computer bags — and then out of nowhere — someone throws up on their shoes and puts a wrinkle into the morning schedule. Others are dealing with a terminally ill partner, relying on public transportation, wrestling with mental health issues, or even suffering from domestic violence. Maybe each employee is just doing the best they can on any given day. Seeing employees as human, as people, not just as a number or replaceable resource, helps us all display more empathy.

During the COVID-19 pandemic, many employees in the service industry, especially airports, hospitals, hotels, and restaurants, opted to move into other careers, leaving a global staff shortage in these important sectors. Most customers and patients understood the restrictions and limitations during the pandemic and as venues first began to open back up. But our memories are short-lived, and our expectations are set back to their pre-pandemic levels, even though the staff is not. One perspective is that we should have greater empathy for those who opted to stay the course in these industries, who are working harder than ever for the same or less salary, often without a full staff in place.

An atypical workplace is a football (soccer) club. The pressure to perform, dealing with fame, risking injury, and keeping up with family life all present unique challenges to this profession. One football club, Liverpool FC, adopted the song "You'll Never Walk Alone" as their mantra. Written in 1963 by a local Liverpool band, Gerry & The Pacemakers, the song serves as a tribute to the fans who were injured and killed during a crowd crush at their stadium in Sheffield in 1989. The football club etched the saying into the iron gates of their stadium as a reminder that all who enter are an essential part of the football club's family.

Most recently, this phrase became the mourning cry for hundreds of thousands around the world when Liverpool footballer, known as Diogo Jota, and his brother, André Silva, who played for FC Penafiel, both died in a car accident on July 3, 2025. Their parents lost both sons, and Jota's wife lost her husband and the father of their three young children. "You'll Never Walk Alone" is the epitome of empathy. It means that even though we're going through tough times, we're not alone on this journey; someone else is putting themselves in our shoes and walking with us. As both coffins left the church in Gondomar in northern Portugal, family members, friends, teammates, and fans walked with them to their final resting place. Liverpool FC showed they were more than a business when they also paid out the remaining two years of Jota's contract to his wife with an additional promise to pay for their children's education, two tangible ways of showing empathy and saying, "You'll Never Walk Alone."

Rereading the quote from Satya Nadella, we would only add one word to it: "Without empathy it is not possible to get the best from your team, so for this reason it is the key (ingredient) to everything." Let's make sure we bring empathy into the workplace and beyond.

Food for Thought

1	It can be scary to be ourselves at work and show that we need empathy.
2	Research shows empathy can improve employee satisfaction and business results.
3	We're all at different stages of our careers; we need to accommodate those differences to share empathy.
4	Who can we reassure today that they will never walk alone?

A Recipe to Share

Ever notice someone at work who eats alone or doesn't get invited out to group lunches? One way to bring everyone together at work is to have a monthly potluck and advertise it well in advance. It's a chance to connect outside of meetings and talk about something other than work.

One of Pam's potluck favorites is the meatball recipe below. This guaranteed crowd-pleaser comes from Pam's sister, who learned it from her mother-in-law.

Ingredients

Meatballs

- 3 lbs. ground beef
- 2 cups instant oats
- 12 oz evaporated milk
- 2 eggs
- ½ cup chopped onions
- ½ tsp garlic salt
- ½ tsp pepper
- 2 tsp chili powder
- 2 tsp salt

Sauce

- 2 cups ketchup
- 2 cups brown sugar (do not pack)
- ½ cup chopped onions
- 2 tbsp liquid smoke
- ½ tsp garlic salt

Preparation

1. Preheat oven to 350°F.
2. Mix all meatball ingredients very well in a large bowl.
3. Form meatballs into 1 ½ inch rounds (trick from Ana: dip your fingers in oil as you roll your meatballs, so the mixture doesn't stick to your fingers) and place in a baking dish.

Note: Do not pre-fry meatballs.

4. Heat the sauce ingredients in a pan over medium heat. Stir until boiling, then pour over meatballs.
5. Bake uncovered for 1 hour on middle rack.

Section 3:
Roadblocks to Empathy

Although we've started on our path to becoming better at showing empathy, there are a couple of roadblocks that make our journey a bumpy one — not just for us, but for others as well. When people begin to open up, our natural tendencies might be to compare their plight to others' or criticize them for their circumstances. Another hazard is overextending ourselves so we're no longer in the right frame of mind or body to offer empathy. Let's look at how to avoid these pitfalls, protecting ourselves and others along the way.

Comparison and Criticism

"Comparison is the thief of joy." – Commonly attributed to Theodore Roosevelt, 26th President of the United States

As others open up to us, our natural tendency is to go directly into problem-solving mode, an approach that isn't helpful if we want to display true empathy. But there are other ways we can damage the situation even further — and that comes in the form of comparison and criticism.

Here's what this looks like. A friend confides in us that she has breast cancer. In our attempt to make her "feel better," we immediately bring up another friend, or a sister, or an aunt, who also was diagnosed with breast cancer. And then we start to list all of the steps the other individual took, and voilà, she is healthy now, so our friend should feel great about her chances. Ugh.

This is unhelpful for a number of reasons. First, instead of listening to our friend, we've started to talk. We're not letting her tell her story, express her fears, ask her questions, or describe her pain. Second, we've skipped over all of this to compare her case to another's. That downplays what our friend is going through — and even normalizes it somewhat. "Oh, so-and-so had cancer, and they're fine now. So, you shouldn't worry." Or, "With my aunt, the doctors caught it way too late, so in a way, you're lucky." While we might not be using those exact words, the message we're conveying is that it's not as serious as they think it is.

Another human frailty is that of criticism. When someone opens up to us, they make themselves vulnerable. Do we think it's helpful to then criticize their predicament or the choices they've made? "I told you that you shouldn't have married that person. I knew this would happen." And veiled criticism sounds like this: "If I were you, I wouldn't put up with that. I would tell him to get out TONIGHT." There's no room for empathy in this situation. In fact, we've made a bad situation worse by adding a lot of unwanted emotions (embarrassment, anxiety, fear, sadness, or guilt) to the mix.

We should leave the ingredients of comparison and criticism out of our serving of empathy. Instead, let's stop, go into listening mode, and when our friend has finished her story, give empathetic responses such as, "I'm sorry you're going through this. I'm glad you told me, and I want you to know I'll be here in whatever way you need."

When we compare and criticize, we make others feel inadequate or unworthy of empathy. It's unfortunate because to share our problems, we expose ourselves and our insecurities. As if that's not hard enough on its own, being compared to others or criticized makes others feel overwhelmed or defeated.

One last ingredient to leave out is our habit of complaining about our own circumstances when others are opening up. It's a sneaky way of comparing: "You should see what's going on with me. My life is a mess." Again, this cheapens the other person's feelings.

Our responsibility in sharing empathy is to take on the other person's perspective, not our own, not someone else's. It's imagining ourselves in the same situation with the same resources, opportunities, and problems as that person. Again, when we practice the art of listening, we will be less likely to commit these errors of comparison, criticism, and complaining.

Food for Thought

1	Comparing someone's problem to that of another downplays the issue.
2	Criticizing someone for their problem makes matters worse.
3	Complaining about our own problem ignores the other person's situation.
4	If we listen, we're less likely to compare, criticize or complain.

A Recipe to Share

Like life, this little appetizer is sweet, savory, and spicy. Make this when a friend pops over for an afternoon or early evening chat. Pair it with a glass of wine or a sparkling drink. If you don't have time to assemble the appetizer, feel free to set up all the ingredients on a platter so you can assemble and chat at the same time.

This recipe came through Pam's friend, Maria, a great listener, who knows how to make people feel welcomed and loved whenever they drop by.

Ingredients

- 1 package crostini (small, toasted bread)
- ¼ wheel Brie, sliced
- 16 oz quince paste, thinly sliced
- 1-2 fresh jalapeños, thinly sliced in rounds
- 1 red onion, sliced in crescents

Preparation

1. Arrange the crostini on a platter and place one slice of Brie on each piece.
2. Place the quince paste slices on top of the Brie.
3. Place the red onion on top of the quince paste.
4. Lastly, place the sliced jalapeños on top of the red onion.
5. Ready to serve.

Empathy Fatigue

"If you burn the candle at both ends, you're not as bright as you think you are." – Often quoted to Pam by her mother, Patricia

In **Bringing Light to a Dark World** in Section 2, we touched briefly on the topic of not getting burned out while being a light to others. This burning the candle at both ends is a pervasive problem in today's "always on" culture, and burnout is a common side effect for those who practice empathy. One of the pitfalls we face is that we can get so focused on the needs of others that we neglect ourselves and our own needs. Sharing another person's burden can weigh us down if we don't take time to replenish our own reserves.

A natural gravitational pull exists between empathetic people and people in need. We might only see another person's problem on the surface at first, not knowing how deep the issue goes or how much time the empathy journey will take. Some empathetic relationships can feel very one-sided, with an empath doing all the giving and the other doing all the taking. How do we avoid going from having a cup that runneth over to one that runs bone dry?

Psychologist Susan Albers, PsyD, discusses the phenomenon of "empathy fatigue" in an article from The Cleveland Clinic. "Empathy fatigue is the emotional and physical exhaustion that happens from caring for people day after day, after day," Dr. Albers explains. "Over time, we start to see people experiencing a sense of numbness and distancing or difficulty continuing to care."

Dr. Albers goes on to recommend the ABC method to combat empathy fatigue, which we love because it's so easy to remember:

- **Awareness** — Acknowledge how we're feeling and show ourselves some self-compassion.
- **Balance** — Maintain other interests besides doing our job and taking care of other people. Practice self-care.
- **Connection** — Connect with others and talk about our feelings, especially with people we trust.

It might seem unnatural to put ourselves first, but if we lose our gift of empathy or become resentful, we can no longer help anyone. During the safety demonstration aboard an aircraft, how many times have we heard, "Put the mask on yourself first before helping others?" When we're incapacitated, we can't help those around us.

Setting boundaries is a good strategy to employ when practicing empathy. Remember how Pam sets aside a certain time or day to spend with a person in need? That gives her time to recharge herself. Setting time constraints is also wise when helping someone new, since, as we mentioned previously, we may only see the surface of someone's problem. It's better to tread lightly than to jump in with both feet.

Other techniques we discovered in our research to combat empathy fatigue were to get out in nature, meditate, exercise, rest and sleep, eat healthy, listen to music, and get some alone time, especially away from those we're helping.

Lastly, we should get rid of any guilt about practicing self-empathy. Our physical and mental state of mind must remain healthy in order to serve. Like the phrase, "Charity begins at home," empathy begins with self.

Food for Thought

1	Empathy fatigue can happen when we care for others day after day.
2	Let's remember our ABCs to combat empathy fatigue: Awareness, Balance, Connection.
3	We shouldn't feel guilty about practicing self-care and setting boundaries.

A Recipe to Share

How about a little pick-me-up dessert in honor of self-care? We do believe in the healing powers of chocolate, so here is a classic that Ana makes from scratch.

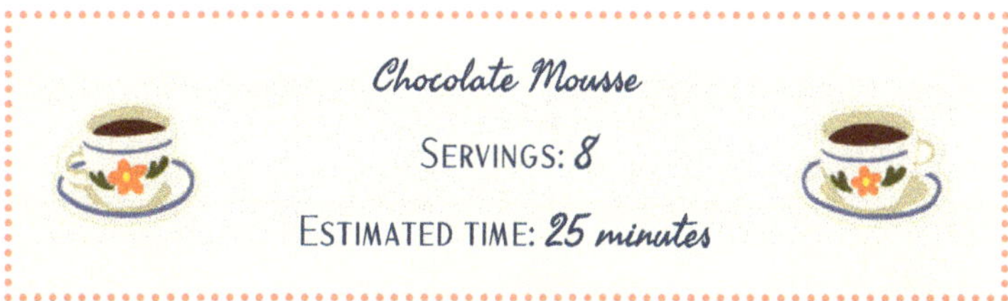

Chocolate Mousse

SERVINGS: *8*

ESTIMATED TIME: *25 minutes*

Ingredients

- 8 oz culinary chocolate
- 6 eggs, separated
- 1 tbsp white sugar
- ¼ cup salted margarine

Preparation

1. Melt the chocolate with margarine in a bain-marie, over medium heat until the chocolate melts. Remove from heat.
2. Beat the egg whites until stiff.

3. Add a spoonful of sugar to the egg yolks and mix with a hand mixer until well beaten.
4. Add the chocolate to the beaten egg whites and mix with a wire whisk.
5. Combine chocolate mixture with egg yolk mixture. Stir carefully by hand.
6. Place equal amounts in individual decorative bowls and refrigerate until served.

Section 4:
Expressing Empathy

Hallmark started a global greeting card business based on our not having the right words for each of life's major milestones or events. Artificial intelligence now writes love letters and thank you notes on our behalf. What makes saying the right thing at the right time so difficult, especially when our intentions are good? If we don't practice effective responses, then we can't express empathy properly. And if we don't change our responses based on context, then our well-meaning words are destructive rather than constructive. Let's take a look at expressing empathy in the right way, at the right time, for the right circumstance.

Empathy's Native Tongue

"Use empathy, thoughtfulness, and kindness in your interactions and think before you speak. A kind word is long remembered." – Cindy Ann Peterson, Author

We've covered the topic of listening more versus talking when showing empathy, but when it comes time to say something, what should those phrases or conversations sound like? We've also discussed what not to say and do. Remember that some people get competitive and start comparing their pain to ours, or they can say the unhelpful things Dr. Brown warned us about, which resemble passing judgment or minimizing the situation.

So, let's talk about what we can and should say, and practice doing this until we become fluent in the language of empathy. Let's look at common scenarios in which empathy is needed, and how the words might change depending on a particular situation. This is a long chapter we've broken into two sections, so feel free to skip to the section that covers what you're dealing with right now.

Part 1 (Death, Health, Crime)

Loss of a Loved One

One of life's most difficult experiences is the loss of a loved one. There's a finality to this situation, and even if we believe in the afterlife, death brings a distinct type of grief. Family members or very close friends may feel a sense of guilt or regret that they didn't do enough for those departed. Or there may be a feeling of relief that the suffering is over, but also guilt associated with that feeling of relief. There may be a fear of the future or a physical, emotional, or financial hardship without this person present. Added to this are the arrangements that need to be handled following a death: contacting family and friends, funeral arrangements, and estate directives.

Here are the words of empathy we can use for someone experiencing the loss of a loved one:

- ✓ "I'm so sorry for your loss."
- ✓ "I want you to know that I am here for you, to help in any way."
- ✓ "I know this is a lot to take in. Is there something I can do for you right now — an errand, grocery shopping, getting a few prepared meals in here?"
- ✓ "I know this must be a shock for you."
- ✓ "Let me know if you want to talk about it. No pressure."

Although nothing we can do or say will change the finality of death, words of empathy can soothe an aching heart. We aren't meant to go through births and deaths on our own. We need one another to get through these major life events.

Health Issue

The old saying, "Health is everything," rings true, as it is challenging to live our lives when we have health problems. When someone close to us gets the dreaded call from their doctor, "I'm sorry to have to let you know that you've been diagnosed with [cancer, Alzheimer's, Parkinson's, fill in the blank]," they can have a lot of different reactions. The same goes for those who have had an accident.

Depending on those reactions, what we say when they share their news with us may vary. Let's go through these examples.

Health Scare

A variety of emotions can come to the surface when someone receives serious news about their health. These can include disbelief, shock, fear, doubt, sadness, despair, frustration, or anger — and these emotions can come and go. For a few, relief might be an emotion that is displayed. As odd as that sounds, for people whose illnesses have stymied medical teams, relief may come after a long-awaited, correct diagnosis and once a treatment plan has been established. The most important things are to let others lead the conversation and for us to react accordingly. If they express . . .

- **Disbelief**, answer: "Yeah, I can't believe this is happening either."
- **Shock**, answer: "This is a shock. I can see how this would be upsetting."
- **Fear**, answer: "I think it's normal to be afraid of this. But I'll be here every step of the way with you."
- **Doubt**, answer: "I think getting a second opinion is wise."
- **Sadness**, answer: "Yeah, this is some pretty tough news. I hear you."
- **Despair**, answer: "I know it's hard to feel hopeful at this time."
- **Frustration**, answer: "I know this wasn't part of the plan. I hope you'll let me help you through this setback."
- **Anger**, answer: "I can understand why you're angry. That would probably be my reaction too."
- **Relief**, answer: "I'm so glad they finally figured out what's going on."

Accident

Depending on the severity of their injuries, it may be some time before we can speak to that person. Remember, in trauma, it's hard to remember all of the details, so our conversations shouldn't be about pumping for information. Rather, we should again see where the other person leads us. It's important to focus on the present day, not the past and not too far into the future. Also, we shouldn't bring up anything that takes away from that person's healing process, i.e., automobile or property damage, medical bills, insurance claims, unless they broach the subject with us first. So, our conversations might sound like this:

- ✓ "How are you feeling today?"
- ✓ "Can I do anything for you, run an errand, bring you something, etc.?"
- ✓ "It looks like you're getting good care in here. Is there anything you need me to ask the nurses for?"
- ✓ "Let me know if you're up for more visits."
- ✓ "What's the best time to visit you?"
- ✓ "Do you need me to call anyone for you?"
- ✓ "I don't mind passing by your house to feed your pets and/or water your plants, if it's okay with you."

Recovery

Recovery can take time for both health scares and accidents. It's important for us to follow up once a person is home; not everything goes back to normal just because someone is discharged or has received treatment. When our loved ones have healed, let's remember to celebrate their recovery with them. In the case of a terminal illness, let's listen to what they need as they approach the end of their lives here on Earth. Pam, along with her family, dear friends, and a hospice team, helped care for her mother after she was diagnosed with pancreatic cancer. One of the things Pam remembers was that soon after they arrived home from the hospital, her mother began listing specific items that she wanted given to various relatives and friends. Pam set up a table with all of the items, along with Post-It® notes with names written on them. It's important to do tasks that are important to the other person when they prefer. At some point, a terminal patient may not be able to communicate as clearly what their wishes are.

A final point in this section is that we shouldn't ignore the caregivers. Caring for others, especially when we don't have formal training, can take a toll. Let's remember to share our empathy with these compassionate people who are making personal sacrifices and to offer to do something for them as well.

Crime Victim

While we don't automatically think of crime victims when we talk about empathy, the reality is that crime exists, and it presents an unexpected crisis for people around us and even ourselves.

People who are criminally victimized also experience similar emotions to those dealing with a health scare or accident. Fear, anxiety, and anger are common. Along with these, there can be a new sense of vulnerability and a loss of confidence. The crime may lead to physical and emotional injuries, as well as financial harm. Here are some dos and don'ts for approaching a loved one who has been the victim of a crime.

Don't ask "Why" questions like these:

- ✗ "Why were you by yourself?"
- ✗ "Why did you go to that part of town?"
- ✗ "Why did you carry your purse that way or your wallet in your back pocket?"
- ✗ "Why did you click on that link?"
- ✗ "Why did you give your personal information online?"
- ✗ "Why did you trust that person?"
- ✗ "Why didn't you call me first?"
- ✗ "Why didn't you check the locks (on your car, in your house, for your desk at work)?"

People who have been victimized already feel low, and questions like these can sound an awful lot like blame for a situation that was ultimately out of their control.

Instead, our conversations should go like this:

✓ "I'm so sorry this happened to you. Are you okay?"
✓ "I'm here for you. Do you want me to come over?"
✓ "What can I do to help you right now?"
✓ "Do you need a place to stay?"
✓ "Do you want someone to go with you to the police?"
✓ "Do you need some cash until you can replace your stolen credit cards?"
✓ "Do you need a ride somewhere until you get your driver's license back?"

Pam was living in an apartment during college when a man tried to break into her home. He was unsuccessful, but even after calling the police, she was still uneasy to stay in the apartment alone. Pam's brother spent the next few nights sleeping on her couch until she felt safe enough to be on her own. That's a tangible example of empathy and love.

Part 2 (Unemployment, Conflict, Isolation)

Loss of Employment

They say money can't buy happiness, but the harsh reality is that without income or a financial lifeline, we can all go downhill pretty quickly. When family members, friends, or colleagues lose a job, their day-to-day routine changes dramatically. Often, they have more time in the day to reflect on their job loss, and this can lead to depression and despair. In addition to providing words of empathy, it's important to check in often and also discuss topics other than the employment search. Many people just can't take another, "Have you found a job yet?" question. None of us should be asking this question; the individual will be sure to share the good news when this occurs.

So, what can we say in this situation?

- ✓ "What can I do to help you?" An open-ended question is a good way to start, and then let the person lead us from there.
- ✓ If they ask for help with the job search, a good response from us would be, "Yes, I'd love to help. What would be most beneficial for you right now?"

This will guide the conversation to discover whether the unemployed person needs help with reviewing a CV or resume, getting an introduction to a shared colleague, looking for opportunities within our own networks, recommending a headhunter or job coach, deciding which additional training might be needed, or finding a new professional organization to join.

Beyond the typical email, social network exchanges, and phone calls, it's also important to set aside some time to take this person out to lunch or dinner or invite them to a fun activity that we pay for. While it can be a little embarrassing at times to lean on others for help, the unemployed also need a chance to get outside of their home environment and engage with others, something that may be cut off without a workplace to go to (physical or virtual). During this dedicated time, we should let the other person talk, leading the conversation in the way they want. It could be a good time for that person to express their fears, concerns, complaints, or progress. On the other hand, the conversation may turn to topics that have nothing to do with job hunting, turning this precious time into a respite from focusing on employment.

Here are some ideas that make the expression of empathy more tangible. How can we help this unemployed person secure some short-term income, if they're open to that idea?

- ✓ Do they need help filling out paperwork to receive unemployment benefits?
- ✓ Do they have assets they can sell but don't know how?

- ✓ Do we have an odd job or project we need help with that we could pay this person for?
- ✓ Do we know about other temporary work that might be outside this person's typical skill set but could be possible?

One time, Pam was laid off from her part-time job while she was attending college. It was difficult to find another job that also worked with her school schedule. Pam's cousin offered her a part-time gig cleaning houses that filled the gap until Pam could find work again. In her case, that was her former company calling her back in to do the same job.

Conflict with Family and Friends

One of the most painful experiences is when we have a conflict with family members and friends. In terms of families, we aren't able to choose the one we were born into, but as we grow older, it's possible to build up a network of friends that can become like family. Society dictates that we're supposed to love our families, but sometimes conflict and emotional pain that are present in those relationships make it difficult for love to thrive. While friends are chosen, conflict can be just as hurtful in these relationships. We can feel guilty or depressed when things don't work as we feel they should.

So, what can we say to those who are experiencing familial and friendship woes?

- ✓ "I'm sorry you're having trouble with [fill in name of family member/friend]. That must be hard."
- ✓ "I can understand why you're upset. That would be upsetting to me, too."
- ✓ "I hope things work out. You're a good [family/friend] to me, and I would be sad if there was conflict between us."

We should avoid speaking ill of others' families and friends. Rather, we can show empathy by helping to fill in the temporary or long-term gap that may arise because of the relationship conflict.

- ✓ "Want to hang out this weekend?"
- ✓ "I was thinking about trying out that new restaurant. Want to join me?"
- ✓ "Hey there, just checking in on you. How's it going? Want to catch up?"

Hopefully, our efforts to show empathy can help present a positive alternative to the negative effects of this type of conflict.

Isolation/New to Town

Our circumstances often change as we go through life. It's not unusual to feel lonely or out of place when big life events occur. While these circumstances may be of our doing, that doesn't mean we're immune to negative feelings. Let's consider a few different scenarios.

New neighbors just moved in next door. It's possible they feel alone or anxious. Maybe the move was brought on by a family member's new job. Could there be someone at home who's trying to navigate a new town or trying to settle in on their own? Our homes are meant to be our sanctuaries, but with unfamiliar surroundings, it can be tough to feel a sense of belonging or peace.

One of the best things we can do to show empathy is to remember how it felt when we were new to the neighborhood ourselves. Maybe it was hard for us to take the initiative to introduce ourselves. With that in mind, we feel it's helpful for us to make the first move, but in a way that's not overwhelming. Here are some examples of what to do and say.

Call out a friendly greeting and approach a new neighbor casually with an introduction — our names and which house/apartment is ours. It's probably a good idea to do this one person at a time; we shouldn't show up with our whole family in tow. If we feel comfortable doing so, have a Post-It note with our name and phone number on it and to encourage new neighbor(s) to call if they need anything.

Another way to welcome someone to the neighborhood is to bring over a small gift — it could be lemons from our yards or a plant. If one of these small interactions leads to a conversation, great. If not, we should be patient and let our new neighbors get comfortable around us and their new neighborhood.

And while we mentioned home being our sanctuaries, for others, it can be a place of isolation and loneliness. We talked about this in **Making Time for Empathy** in Section 2. Let's consider our elderly neighbors whose children have grown and moved far away, or people with disabilities that limit their ability to interact with others or get out of the house. The days can be very long for these people, and the nights even longer. Showing empathy for this situation can come in a few forms. It's not just with words, but it's accompanied by in-person contact.

Ana visits her elderly parents every Sunday. This gives them a regular schedule to plan a family meal and gives her parents something to look forward to all week. The parents also know this is a good time to review letters and bills they may have trouble understanding and discuss small repairs that need to be done. This is clearly empathy in action, more than words, a physical presence of love and help. Things the isolated, elderly, and lonely are missing include a kind word, a hug, someone who remembers their special milestones, or a sympathetic ear to hear their everyday woes.

Dan Buettner, author of *Blue Zones: Lessons for Living Longer from the People Who've Lived the Longest*, and his team have studied several societies that subscribe to a certain way of living. One of the key components is how a village honors and cares for their elderly. One example cited is the Okinawans, who live longer than people in many other places, with fewer cases of cancer, heart disease, and dementia on average. Elderly community members are prioritized by people of all ages as social and practical concerns. Instead of pushing the elderly to one side, our empathetic attitudes should include them in daily activities, not only driving depression and disease away, but also setting up a model for how we want to be treated as we age.

One of the key initiatives discussed in the *Blue Zones* book is to create a strong social network, one that is face-to-face instead of online, with "a lifelong circle of friends that supports people well into old age." This creation of a strong social network happens over a period of years. The network can include members of our church, our former classmates, our neighborhood, our walking group, our clubs (book club, cooking club, sewing club, sports club, etc.), or people we volunteer with. Who are the people who will notice when things aren't quite right with us at any given time, or who will call us when we don't show up for our normal activities? Beyond family members who could be far away or gone, this circle of friends keeps an eye on one another and removes the risk of isolation.

Food for Thought

1	Knowing the right words to express empathy takes practice and contextual awareness.
2	Empathy in action is volunteering to help others in practical ways.
3	Developing a strong social network can give us built-in people to share empathy.
4	Before showing empathy to another, read the section of this chapter that applies to that person's situation.

A Recipe to Share

Choosing the right words can make the difference between helping and harming someone. It's like selecting the right almonds for our next recipe.

Did you know that bitter almonds are poisonous because they contain high levels of amygdalin, which converts to cyanide? Sweet almonds are safe to eat and are what is sold in grocery stores.

Ingredients

Dough

- ½ cup white sugar
- 3 eggs
- ¾ cup flour
- ½ cup margarine, melted and slightly cooled
- 1 tsp baking powder

Cream

- ⅔ cup sliced almonds
- ½ cup white sugar
- ½ cup margarine
- Scant ½ cup milk

Preparation

1. Preheat the oven to 350°F
2. Mix the sugar with the eggs, then add the flour, baking powder, and margarine until combined.

3. Grease the pan with margarine, sprinkle with flour, and add the dough.
4. Bake for 20 minutes.
5. Add all the cream ingredients to a pan and heat on high until caramelized.
6. Pour over the baked tart and return to the oven until the cream turns golden.
7. Ready to serve.

Section 5:

Building, Sharing, and Receiving Empathy

Research shows that communities that build empathy into their daily lives help people live longer, happier, and healthier lives. Part of this building process requires us to give of ourselves, becoming transparent enough to share what's going on with us and also being vulnerable and humble enough to be on the receiving end of empathy. It's a full circle that falls apart if we don't embrace this part of our humanity.

The Data Behind Empathy

"Familiarity, visibility and accountability are the ingredients of empathy's primordial soup." – Dr. Jamil Zaki, Professor at Stanford University and Author

We've covered a lot in the previous chapters — what empathy is, and what it's not, how to listen more than we speak, how to make time for empathy and put it into action, how to protect ourselves as empaths, and what to say and not say, depending on the situation. Instinctively, we know that empathy is a good thing, and we also have a feeling that people are less empathetic than they used to be.

But what data exists to validate these instincts and feelings? Dr. Jamil Zaki is a professor of psychology at Stanford University and the director of the Stanford Social Neuroscience Lab. He trained at Columbia and Harvard, studying empathy and kindness in the human brain. In his online presentation, *Building Empathy in a Fractured World*, he discusses how "decades of evidence now demonstrate countless ways that empathy benefits everyone involved, including ourselves."

In an excerpt from this presentation, Dr. Zaki outlines these benefits:

- **Self**: Individuals who feel empathy report being happier, experiencing less depression and stress, and having an easier time forming and keeping important relationships. They're also more likely to succeed professionally.
- **Others**: Patients of empathic doctors are more satisfied with their care, employees of empathic managers are less likely

to call in sick with stress-related illnesses, and spouses of empathic partners report being happier in their marriages.

- **Community**: People who feel lots of empathy also tend to help strangers by volunteering and donating to charities. Empathy also makes it less likely for them to engage with stereotyping, prejudice, and bias.

Dr. Zaki then explains why showing empathy in today's world is more difficult. Early humans lived in small communities, where there was an abundance of "familiarity, visibility, and accountability." He views these key components as "ingredients of social life as empathy's primordial soup, making it easy and natural for us to connect with and care about one another." He summarizes the reasons why our civilization has become less empathetic by many of us having moved away from our small communities and their social activities, into large cities, often doing things on our own, online, and anonymously.

Psychologists have compiled the results of a self-reported study on empathy, developed by Konrath et al., in 2011. In this study, Americans responded to twenty-eight statements to determine their "Empathy Index" on a scale of one to five, with one being the least empathetic and five being the most. In 1979, the average score was four out of five. Thirty years later, in 2009, that average score dropped to three out of five, a 20 percent drop.

The data, statistics, and science behind empathy could make us feel sad about its current trajectory. But Dr. Zaki asks a very fundamental question: "Does it have to be this way?" The answer is "No."

According to the Centers for Disease Control and Prevention (CDC), people with stronger social bonds have a 50 percent increased likelihood of survival compared to those who have fewer social connections. When we're socially connected and care about each other, we make better decisions that affect our health, and we're less likely to suffer from stress, anxiety, and depression. When we belong to a community, it's easier to find and give empathy because we're a part of one another's lives, and we know what's going on.

Let's also consider additional research from Dan Buettner, author of *The Blue Zones Secrets for Living Longer*, that shows some commonalities among places where people live longer, happier lives. In these zones people tend to move naturally (walking, moving, doing daily chores but also taking time to rest and recharge), to have a positive outlook (through their religion or culture), to eat wisely (natural versus processed foods, not overeating), and to connect (socially, with family and friends, with a sense of community).

We can't control other people's decisions around how often they move, what they eat, or their outlook, but we can help with making connections. We have the ability to provide social, emotional, psychological, and physical benefits to other humans by connecting with empathy and providing them with a sense of belonging. Let's change the empathy trajectory together.

Food for Thought

1	Data shows that empathy benefits us, others, and the broader community.
2	Familiarity, visibility and accountability are all key factors of groups with high levels of empathy.
3	Empathy suffers when we don't have close human connections and when we do more online and anonymously.

A Recipe to Share

As we mentioned, we can't control what others eat, but as a nod to healthy eating habits, we've included this vegan, gluten-free dish that Ana often cooks for those with dietary restrictions.

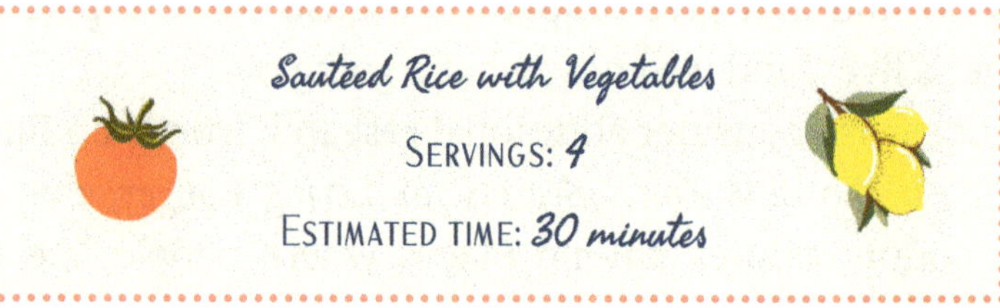

Sautéed Rice with Vegetables

SERVINGS: 4

ESTIMATED TIME: 30 minutes

Ingredients

- Olive oil
- ½ red bell pepper, cut into long, thin strips
- ½ green bell pepper, cut into long, thin strips
- ½ yellow bell pepper, cut into long, thin strips
- ½ zucchini, diced
- ½ onion, diced
- 1 carrot, cut into long, thin strips
- 1 head broccoli, cut into small pieces
- 3 white mushrooms, sliced
- 1 ½ cups of cooked white rice
- Tamari (gluten-free soy sauce)
- 6 cherry tomatoes, cut into halves
- Handful of chopped parsley

Preparation

1. Add a drizzle of olive oil to a wok and heat on high.
2. Add all the vegetables to the wok and sauté for at least 5 minutes.
3. Then add the cooked rice and let it fry a little.
4. To finish, add tamari to taste and sauté while continuing to stir.
5. Serve with chopped parsley and cherry tomatoes.

Sharing Our Stories

"If we can share our story with someone who responds with empathy and understanding, shame can't survive." – Dr. Brené Brown

Storytelling is as old as humanity itself. It's a tool that connects us to each other and our common experiences. Telling our stories is good for the soul, and keeping our thoughts, hopes, and fears bottled up causes internal turmoil.

But when it's time to share our stories, we often hold back. Maybe we feel ashamed or foolish, and we fear judgment. These feelings and fears are normal; it can be difficult to find someone who will listen with empathy and understanding.

In order to tell our stories, we have to let down our guards and become vulnerable. As the words come out in the presence of empathy, we no longer carry the burden alone. Any given story can become the recipe of healing for someone else. Others often benefit from learning how we handled a certain situation, how we felt, and how things turned out.

Ana and Pam share stories with each other as mothers of adult children. Remember that empathy and understanding can be easier to find in someone with similar experiences. It's easy to feel judged for our parenting skills by those who aren't parents. In the same way, it requires extra empathy for us to understand what men go through, as we're not men. The same goes for connecting with other races, cultures, age groups, education levels, etc., that differ from our own backgrounds. It doesn't mean all the parties involved aren't empathetic; it just means we may have to put more effort into learning about different perspectives through others.

Sharing our stories lets other people know that we're all doing the best we can, that life isn't easy, and that problems are things that can be shared, not just handled on our own.

And to hit home the point about the importance of owning problems together, here's a story by children's book author, Mark Transki, edited for brevity here:

> *"A mouse, looking through a hole in the wall, sees the farmer and his wife open a package. He was terrified to see that it was a mousetrap. He ran to the patio to warn everyone. "There is a mousetrap at home!"*
> *The chicken said, "Excuse me, Mr. Mouse. I understand that's a big problem for you, but it doesn't hurt me at all."*
> *So, the rodent went to the lamb who replied the same way, "Excuse me, Mr. Mouse, but I don't think I can do anything more than pray for you."*
> *The mouse went to the cow, and she said, "But am I in danger? I think not!"*
> *The mouse returned to the house, worried and dejected to face the farmer's mousetrap. That night a great noise was heard like that of the mousetrap catching its victim. The farmer's wife ran to see what she had caught. In the dark she did not see that the mousetrap had caught the tail of a poisonous snake. The speedy snake bit the woman. The farmer immediately took her to the hospital, and she came back with a high fever.*
> *The farmer, to comfort her, prepared a nutritious soup. He grabbed the knife and went to find the main ingredient: the chicken. Since the woman did not get better, friends and neighbors went to visit them. The farmer killed the lamb to feed them. The woman did not get better and died.*
> *And in the end, the husband sold the cow to the slaughterhouse to cover the funeral expenses."*

The next time someone tells us about their problem, we should treat it as our problem, too. In the area of Portugal where Ana and Pam live, many who are employed in the service industry struggle to make ends meet even though the region is prosperous. We could shake this off as someone else's problem, but in truth, it's everyone's problem. Without the service industry in our area, the restaurants would shut down, stores would close, house cleaners and gardeners would work elsewhere, schools would have fewer teachers and students, and life, in general, would be less diverse and more difficult.

The financial struggles of service employees will come to our front door if we don't help. This help can come in the form of leaving generous tips, paying higher-than-average wages for those services, giving a break on rents, and just listening, with empathy and understanding.

What story do we need to tell or hear today in our journey of empathy? Let's take up Dr. Brown's challenge and respond with empathy and understanding, so shame finds no haven when stories are shared.

Food for Thought

1	Sharing our stories requires being vulnerable but is an important element of empathy.
2	It's easier to share stories with those who have "walked in our shoes."
3	Often, we believe that other people's problems won't affect us, but their situations can very much affect our lives.

A Recipe to Share

This chicken dish imitates life; it's both sweet and sour. Empathy means being there for others during the "sour" moments.

Sweet and Sour Chicken

SERVINGS: 4-6

ESTIMATED TIME: 40 minutes

Ingredients

- 3 tsp sunflower oil
- 4 chicken breasts, diced
- Salt and pepper
- ¼ cup 1 tbsp grated ginger
- 1 red bell pepper, diced
- 1 green bell pepper, diced
- 2 onions, chopped
- 8 oz can cut pineapple in syrup
- 4 tbsp vinegar
- 1 tsp cornstarch
- Soy sauce (or tamari) to taste

Preparation

1. Season the chicken pieces with salt, pepper, and ginger.
2. In a large frying pan, heat the oil over high heat and pan fry the chicken until golden.
3. Add both peppers and onions and fry well.
4. Add the pineapple pieces (save the syrup) and mix them with the chicken. Continue frying.
5. In a separate bowl, mix half of the pineapple syrup with the vinegar, cornstarch, and soy sauce.
6. Add the syrup mixture to the sautéed chicken and bring to a boil.
7. Reduce the heat and stir until thickened.
8. Serve immediately with rice.

Receiving Empathy

"We need to receive empathy to give empathy."
– Marshall B. Rosenberg, Ph.D., American psychologist, mediator, author, and teacher

Now we're turning the tables from showing and giving empathy to being on the receiving end of this wonderful gift. It should be natural to welcome something we often crave, right? Believe it or not, this is not as easy as it sounds.

To receive empathy means we've had to be vulnerable enough to share our story with someone else in the hopes that it was heard without judgment or a lack of understanding. That vulnerability opens up a barrier which we invite another person to cross. Will that person think of us differently now that we've shown our weakness?

The ability to receive empathy takes strength and, for some, means pushing aside old habits. Many of us were told to pull ourselves up by our bootstraps when faced with a problem. Or we were raised to keep our needs private, as not to burden others. Maybe we were even made to feel that we're not worthy of being listened to or helped. But empathy, as we've seen in previous chapters, is good for our physical and emotional well-being. By receiving empathy, we're also helping to build that skill in others.

In an article titled "Why Is It So Hard To Ask For Help?" Laurie Leinwand, MA, LPC, and Topic Expert Contributor for

GoodTherapy® talks about the barriers and benefits of asking for help, paraphrased here:

- We feel stress when we're not as productive as we think we should be, but we can move forward by asking for help when we're stuck.
- We fear rejection if we ask others for help, but we can collaborate and lean on the skill sets of others to fill in our gaps.
- We feel like impostors when we don't know it all, but we can learn from others so we can use those new resources going forward.

Leinwand talks about how sometimes we all get "stuck," and we must become vulnerable to ask for help, and in doing so we may learn new skills in the process. Pam remembers when her father was remodeling their childhood home. He was doing a lot of it on his own, and he began to lose motivation, causing a long break in the schedule. He had a neighbor who had lost his job but knew a lot about construction, and Pam's dad asked if he could hire him to help with the house. The neighbor quickly agreed. The next day, they made a lot of headway, with the neighbor showing Pam's dad some tricks of the trade. That same evening, the neighbor's employer called offering him his former job back, and he accepted. He called Pam's dad, who was happy for him. The amazing thing was that even one day of help gave Pam's dad the inspiration to keep going on the project and some more efficient ways to get the job done. And the two neighbors became closer because of this single event. Pam's dad made himself vulnerable and asked for help, which resulted in multiple positive results.

As we age, our view of empathy may change. By the time we become older adults, we will have experienced more life events and so can relate more easily to others with similar experiences. Many of us have been in the role of caretaker for children or for chronically ill or aging family members. It may be difficult for some of us to accept the fact that it has become our turn to be cared for. Developing and modeling empathy, especially in front of our children, who may one day be responsible for our care, is a good way to prepare for receiving empathy.

While a study summarized by Jeewon Oh in a 2020 article shows that empathy generally increases with age, particularly after age forty, it also points to a decrease when there are cognitive issues. In that case, the research shows, "Aging also presents cognitive challenges, making it harder for some older people to take other people's perspectives, and thereby lowering empathy."

On the whole, receiving empathy is an important ingredient in our overall well-being. But a word of caution to our readers: Being successful in getting empathy has a lot to do with asking the right people at the right time. Calling others in the middle of their work schedule, during dinner, when they're on vacation, or when they're dealing with their own crisis might not yield the best results for being listened to and empathized with.

Food for Thought

1	The irony of receiving empathy is that we need strength to share our weaknesses.
2	Benefits of receiving empathy include getting unstuck, collaborating with others, and learning new skills.
3	We need to consider carefully of whom, when, and where we expect to receive empathy.

A Recipe to Share

We can learn a lot from others, especially our older generations. Ever wonder why our grandparents always seemed to have a jar or pocket full of hard candy? It could be the secret to making them such good listeners, and when they do speak, it's usually with sweetness and wisdom. Ana's recipe has been passed down from previous generations.

Grandma's Candy

SERVINGS: *8-10*

ESTIMATED TIME: *20 minutes to prepare; 1 hour to chill*

Ingredients

- 8 oz condensed milk
- 8 oz regular whole milk
- 4 eggs, separated
- 1 tbsp instant coffee
- Tea biscuits
- ¼ cup white sugar
- 1 cup heavy cream

Preparation

1. Cook the condensed and regular milk with the egg yolks in a pan, stirring continuously until thickened.
2. Prepare the coffee with a little cold water. Then soak the biscuits in the coffee.
3. On a tray, fill the bottom with the coffee-soaked biscuits.
4. Remove the milk mixture from the stove and pour it over the biscuits.

5. In a bowl, beat the egg whites and sugar with a hand mixer until stiff.
6. Whip the heavy cream and mix it with the egg whites.
7. Place it on top of the biscuits and refrigerate for 1 hour.
8. Decorate with biscuits broken into pieces or crushed, depending on your taste

Wrap Up & Quick Tips

We've arrived at the end of our empathy journey, where we just want to offer a "Pay it Forward" challenge to begin putting our newly developed skills around empathy into practice. We've also included some quick tips that can help us as we develop our empathy skills.

Paying It Forward

"Paying it forward is an expense we all can afford and one that humanity can't afford to live without." - Anonymous

We covered a lot of ground in a short period of time. When we look back, we remember the four key ingredients of empathy outlined by Dr. Teresa Wiseman: 1) taking on someone else's perspective, 2) being nonjudgmental, 3) recognizing someone else's emotion or understanding their feelings, and 4) communicating your understanding of a person's feelings.

If each of us did just those four things, the world would already be a more empathetic place to live and thrive. If we remember to make time for empathy, listen more than we speak, and when we do, use words that help versus harm, our efforts will go even further.

So now it's time to take everything we've learned and put it into action. When we wait for others to show empathy, we could be waiting a long time. Let's instead lead the way. Starting with one person in your life, take time to practice the art of empathy, listening to their story, without judging, without problem-solving, without comparing or criticizing. We believe this will have a multiplier effect. Our households will be happier, our communities will be happier, our society will be happier, and the world will change.

It starts with one person at a time. Each of us is a key ingredient to spreading empathy. Remember the words of Roy T. Bennett, "Always have a willing hand to help someone, you might be the only one that does."

Please share your story with us. We're here to listen.

Quick Tips

1. When a friend shares a problem, we might:

   ✗ Go into problem-solving mode.
   ✗ Judge, criticize, compare with others.
   ✗ Think that the problem is theirs alone.

   Instead, try to:

   ✓ Listen, trying to understand the other's perspective.
   ✓ Listen without judgment, offering words of empathy.
   ✓ Realize that we're all connected, and others' problems can also affect us.

2. When we get empathy fatigue, we might:

   ✗ Ignore our own needs and put others' needs ahead of our own.

   Instead, we should:

   ✓ Take time and space to recharge; become aware, restore balance, and connect with others.

3. When we ask caregivers how they are, we might:

   ✗ Take a caregiver's attitude at face value.
   ✗ Believe everything is "fine" if they say so.

   Instead, we should:

   ✓ Remember that caregivers tend to deprioritize their own problems.
   ✓ Look for ways to help caregivers and give them a chance to share their burdens.

4. When we hesitate to ask for help, we might:

   ✗ Suffer in silence, being too embarrassed or proud to ask.
   ✗ Not want to seem inferior or unknowledgeable.
   ✗ Not expect empathy, not having received it from others in the past.

We should:

- ✓ Learn to be vulnerable and remember we all need empathy.
- ✓ Be open to learning a new skill or a better way of doing things.
- ✓ Remember to talk to others when they're not in the middle of something.
- ✓ Be open to talking to someone else if your usual support isn't working.

5. When we're unsure how to get started in sharing empathy, we might:

- ✗ Think only big gestures will demonstrate our empathy.
- ✗ Be afraid of not being qualified.

We should:

- ✓ Start small, such as running an errand, making a meal, or meeting for coffee.
- ✓ Simply listen.

Food for Thought

1	Getting good at empathy requires a lot of listening and walking in someone else's shoes.
2	We don't have to perform empathy on a grand scale; even helping one person causes a multiplier effect.
3	Developing human connections and relationships enables empathy to survive.
4	We have the same "twenty-four-hour rule" as everyone else. Let's make the most of each day and be the light that someone else needs to get through theirs.

A Recipe to Share

Some of us are amateurs when it comes to cooking and baking, but with Ana's help, we can all become better cooks, one recipe at a time. Here is her version of Apple Pie. Enjoy!

Apple Pie

SERVINGS: 8

ESTIMATED TIME: 40 minutes

Ingredients

- 2 eggs
- ½ cup + 2 tbsp white sugar
- ½ cup + 2 tbsp flour
- 6 tbsp whole milk
- 5 tbsp oil
- 1 pinch salt
- Unsalted butter
- Apples with skin on, thinly sliced
- Cinnamon, as desired

Preparation

1. Preheat the oven to 350°F. Grease a pie pan with butter and sprinkle with flour.
2. Add eggs, sugar, flour, milk, oil, and salt in a bowl and beat very well.
3. Place the mixture in the greased pie pan.
4. Place overlapping apple slices on top, circling the pan until mixture is completely covered.
5. Dust with cinnamon and place in the oven for 20 minutes.

Resources

Recommended Reading

- *The Blue Zones Kitchen: 100 Recipes to Live to 100* by Dan Buettner
- *The Gifts of Imperfection: Let Go of Who You Think You're Supposed to Be and Embrace Who You Are* by Brené Brown
- *Multipliers: How the Best Leaders Make Everyone Smarter* by Liz Wiseman
- *Dignity: Its Essential Role in Resolving Conflict* by Donna Hicks, Ph.D.
- *Crucial Conversations: Tools for Talking When the Stakes Are High* by Kerry Patterson, Joseph Grenny, Ron McMillan, and Al Switzler

Bibliography

Key Ingredients of Empathy

Zorn, Eric. "In All My Years, 50 Things That I've Discovered." *Chicago Tribune* (Chicago), January 3, 2008, 6.

"Brené Brown on Empathy." Video, 2:53. YouTube. Posted by The RSA, December 10, 2013. https://www.youtube.com/watch?v=1Evwgu369Jw.

Wiseman, Theresa. "A concept analysis of empathy." *Journal of Advanced Nursing* 23 (1996): 1162-67.

Everyone Is a Pedestrian

Obama, Barack. "Obama Holds a Town Hall in Istanbul." Address, April 7, 2009. *Washington Post*. https://www.washingtonpost.com/wp-dyn/content/article/2009/04/07/AR2009040701

Obama, Barack. "University of Massachusetts at Boston Commencement Address." Speech, UMass Boston, June 2, 2006.

"Carl Rogers' Core Conditions." Counselling Tutor. https://counsellingtutor.com/counselling-approaches/person-centred-approach-to-counselling/carl-roger

Wheatley, Margaret. "Listening as Healing." *Shambhala Sun*. Last modified December 2001. https://margaretwheatley.com/wp-content/uploads/2014/12/Listening-as-Healing.pdf.

Bringing Light to a Dark World

Williamson, Marianne. *A Year of Miracles: Daily Devotions and Reflections*. HarperOne, 2013.

Ten Boom, Corrie. *The Hiding Place*. Chosen Books, 1971.

Making Time for Empathy

Covey, Stephen R. *Everyday Greatness*. Thomas Nelson, 2009.

Noice, Cathy. "'If you judge people, you have no time to love them.' — Mother Teresa." Workplace Navigator. Last modified January 19, 2018. https://workplacenavigator.com/2018/01/19/if-you-judge-people-you-have-no-time-to-love-them-mother-teresa/.

Empathy in the Workplace

Miller, Hannah L. "What is Empathy? Data Says it's the Leadership Skill Needed Most." Editorial. Leaders. https://leaders.com/articles/leadership/what-is-empathy/.

EY. "New EY US Consulting study: employees overwhelmingly expect empathy in the workplace, but many say it feels disingenuous." News release. March 30, 2023. https://www.ey.com/en_us/newsroom/2023/03/new-ey-us-consulting-study.

Ross, Maria. "How The Empathy Gap Became A $180 Billion Organizational Problem." *Forbes*, July 29, 2025. https://www.forbes.com/sites/mariaross/2025/07/29/how-the-empathy-gap-became-a-180-billion-organizational-problem/.

Sinek, Simon. *Leaders Eat Last*. Penguin Books Limited, 2014.

Longdon, Victoria. "How did 'You'll Never Walk Alone' become Liverpool Football Club's anthem?" Classic FM. Last modified March 14, 2023. https://www.classicfm.com/discover-music/youll-never-walk-alone-liverpool-fc/.

Comparison and Criticism

"Theodore Roosevelt > Quotes > Quotable Quote." Goodreads. https://www.goodreads.com/quotes/6471614-comparison-is-the-thief-of-joy

Empathy Fatigue

"Empathy Fatigue: How Stress and Trauma Can Take a Toll on You." Cleveland Clinic. Last modified June 25, 2021. https://health.clevelandclinic.org/empathy-fatigue-how-stress-and-trauma-can-take-a-toll-on-you.

Empathy's Native Tongue

Peterson, Cindy Ann, Yasmin Anderson-Smith, Laura Barclay, et al. *The Power of Civility: Top Experts Reveal the Secrets to Social Capital*. THRIVE Publishing, 2011.

Buettner, Dan. *The Blue Zones: Lessons for Living Longer from the People Who've Lived the Longest*. National Geographic Society, 2010.

The Data Behind Empathy

Zaki, Jamil. *The War for Kindness: Building Empathy in a Fractured World*. Crown, 2019.

Konrath, Sara, Alison Jane Martingano, Mark Davis, and Fritz Breithaupt. "Empathy Trends in American Youth Between 1979 and 2018: An Update." *Social Psychological and Personality Science*.

"Social Connection." CDC. Last modified May 15, 2024. https://www.cdc.gov/social-connectedness/about/index.html.

Buettner, Dan. *The Blue Zones Secrets for Living Longer*. Disney Publishing Group, 2023.

Sharing Our Stories

Brown, Brené. *Daring Greatly: How the Courage to Be Vulnerable Transforms the Way We Live, Love, Parent, and Lead*. Penguin Publishing Group, 2012.

Transki, Mark. "The Story of a Mouse who live with a Cow, Pig, and Chicken in a Farm." Mark Transki (blog), December 17, 2015. https://marktranski.wordpress.com/2015/12/17/the-story-of-a-mouse-who-live-with-a-cow-pig-and-chicken-in-a-farm/.

Receiving Empathy

Rosenberg, Marshall B., and Deepak Chopra. *Nonviolent Communication: A Language of Life*. PuddleDancer Press, 2015.

Leinwand, Laurie. "Why Is It So Hard to Ask for Help?" Good Therapy. Last modified June 16, 2016. https://www.goodtherapy.org/blog/why-is-it-so-hard-to-ask-for-help-0616164.

Oh, Jeewon. "Do We Become More Empathic as We Get Older?" *Character and Context Blog*. https://spsp.org/news-center/character-context-blog/do-we-become-more-empathic-we-get-older.

Paying It Forward

Jonas, Laurie. "How to Create a Ripple Effect of Paying It Forward." *Living Marvelously* (blog), September 24, 2019. https://livingmarvelously.com/ripple-effect-of-paying-it-forward/.

Bennett, Roy T. *The Light in the Heart*. 2020.

Recipe Index

Starters

- Maria's Appetizer, 41
- Scrambled Eggs with Farinheira and Tomato, 23
- Aunt May's Miracle Meatballs, 33

Mains

- Sautéed Linguini with Shrimp and Cherry Tomatoes, 11
- Lucy's Fish, 16
- Salted Codfish Casserole "Gomes de Sá", 27
- Sautéed Rice with Vegetables, 70
- Sweet and Sour Chicken, 74,

Desserts

- Chocolate Mousse, 45
- Almond Tart, 62
- Grandma's Candy, 78
- Apple Pie, 86

Note: See all recipes again at the end of the book.

Acknowledgments

Ana and Pam would like to thank, first and foremost, their families, where empathy finds itself in everyday examples. Although several family members have passed on, we take great responsibility in sharing this legacy of empathy. We would also like to thank the publishers, editors, and illustrators of How2Conquer for their willingness to bring our story to life and to print.

About the Authors

Ana Lúcia Correia

Ana Lúcia was raised in a small fishing village in Portugal that later became a popular tourist town, where she applied her skills as a chef in the local restaurants. With a heart for people, Ana has always looked out for those who need a helping hand. She demonstrates her love through cooking and makes time for her family, which she has always prioritized. Although she has not traveled extensively, she's delighted to know that her words and recipes will reach beyond and within the borders of Portugal.

Pam Gonçalves

Pam Gonçalves has worked for over thirty years in high-tech companies, where in addition to running marketing, she collaborated with HR teams to develop key employee programs and internal communications. Through her work, Pam helped create positive work cultures and led courses for employees to develop their soft skills. She's also worked as a teacher, mentor, and sounding board.

But first and foremost, Pam is a wife to António (Tony) of over thirty-six years, and they share three amazing adult children. Pam and Tony know the journey of losing their parents and siblings, as well as living in different countries and the challenges that this brings.

Using humor and her genuine love for her community, Pam tries to model empathy in every personal and professional setting.

Recipes

Starters

Maria's Appetizer

SERVINGS: *12*

ESTIMATED TIME: *20 minutes*

Ingredients

- 1 package crostini (small, toasted bread)
- ¼ wheel Brie, sliced
- 16 oz quince paste, thinly sliced
- 1-2 fresh jalapeños, thinly sliced in rounds
- 1 red onion, sliced in crescents

Preparation

1. Arrange the crostini on a platter and place one slice of Brie on each piece.
2. Place the quince paste slices on top of the Brie.
3. Place the red onion on top of the quince paste.
4. Lastly place the sliced jalapeños on top of the red onion.
5. Ready to serve.

Scrambled Eggs with Farinheira and Tomato

SERVINGS: 3

ESTIMATED TIME: 20 minutes

Ingredients

- Olive oil
- ½ ripe tomato, diced
- ½ farinheira sausage (or pork sausage if unavailable)
- 1 chili pepper, sliced in rounds
- 3 eggs
- Salt
- Parsley

Preparation

1. Cut the farinheira in half and remove the skin.
2. Add a little olive oil to a pan and bring to a heat.
3. Add the tomatoes and farinheira and let everything braise.
4. Beat the eggs with a fork and add to the mixture.
5. Stir until eggs are cooked and remove from the heat.
6. Chop some parsley and place on top of the eggs.
7. It's ready to serve.

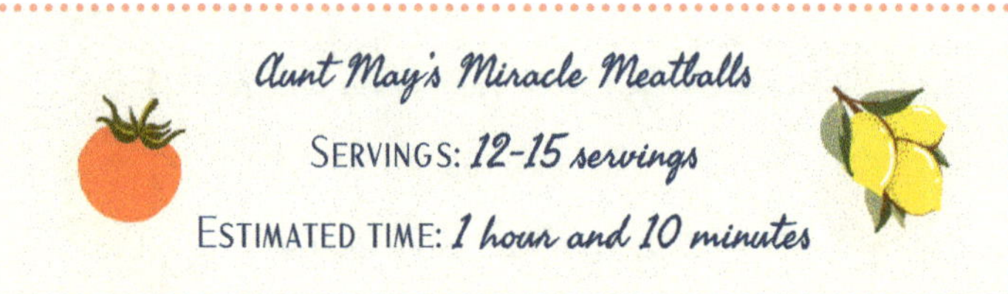

Aunt May's Miracle Meatballs

SERVINGS: *12-15 servings*

ESTIMATED TIME: *1 hour and 10 minutes*

Ingredients

Meatballs

- 3 lbs. ground beef
- 2 cups instant oats
- 12 oz evaporated milk
- 2 eggs
- ½ cup chopped onions
- ½ tsp garlic salt
- ½ tsp pepper
- 2 tsp chili powder
- 2 tsp salt

Sauce

- 2 cups ketchup
- 2 cups brown sugar (do not pack)
- ½ cup chopped onions
- 2 tbsp liquid smoke
- ½ tsp garlic salt

Preparation

1. Preheat oven to 350°F.
2. Mix all meatball ingredients very well in a large bowl.
3. Form meatballs into 1 ½ inch rounds (trick from Ana: dip your fingers in oil as you roll your meatballs, so the mixture doesn't stick to your fingers) and place in a baking dish.

Note: Do not pre-fry meatballs.

4. Heat the sauce ingredients in a pan over medium heat. Stir until boiling, then pour over meatballs.
5. Bake uncovered for 1 hour on middle rack.

Mains

SERVINGS: *4*

ESTIMATED TIME: *30 minutes*

Ingredients

- 1 ½ cups linguini
- 3 tbsp olive oil
- ¼ cup margarine
- 3 cloves garlic, crushed
- 1 bay leaf
- 1 small chili pepper, broken in half
- 1 tsp sweet pepper powder
- 20 shrimp, peeled and deveined
- Salt and pepper
- 1 tbsp brandy
- 1 tbsp white wine
- 10 cherry tomatoes, leave whole
- Grated Parmesan cheese
- Chopped parsley

Preparation

1. Cook the linguini in salted water to package instructions. Ana prefers to cook this "al dente."
2. Sauté garlic in a wok with olive oil and margarine.
3. Add the bay leaf, chili pepper, and sweet pepper powder.

4. Once the garlic browns, add the shrimp. Season with salt and pepper.
5. Drain the linguini, saving some of the water.
6. Continue to sauté the shrimp mixture and add the brandy and white wine. Let it flame a little and add the cherry tomatoes to the middle of the pan.
7. Add the linguini to the shrimp with a little of the linguini cooking water. Sauté for 2 to 3 minutes to absorb the flavor of the shrimp.
8. Remove from the heat and plate the dish to your liking.
9. Serve with Parmesan cheese and chopped parsley.

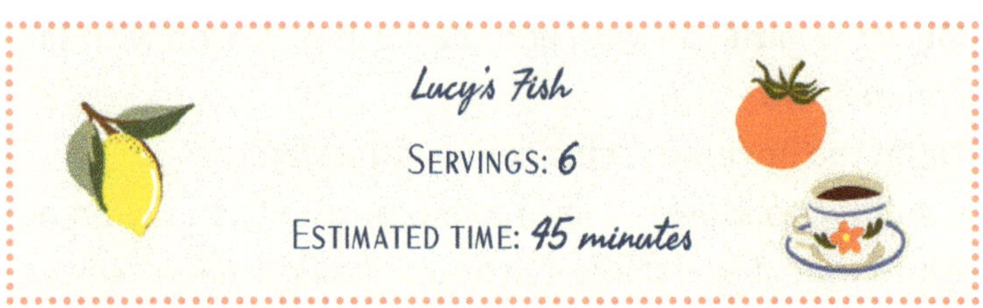

Ingredients

- Olive oil
- 4 medium onions, cut in wedges
- 2 garlic cloves, chopped
- 1 chili pepper, whole
- ½ red bell pepper, cut in rounds
- ½ green bell pepper, cut in rounds
- 8 oz canned peeled tomatoes
- 1 bay leaf
- White wine
- 6 pieces of white fish (croaker recommended, or sea bass)
- 1 oz whiskey
- Soy sauce
- Oregano
- Parsley, chopped

Preparation

1. In a pan, add a drizzle of olive oil and the onion. Heat on high until lightly browned.
2. Add the garlic, chili pepper, and bell peppers.
3. After letting it brown a little, add the peeled tomatoes, bay leaf, and white wine. Lower the heat and simmer for 15 minutes.
4. Salt the fish, add it to the pan, and cook for 10 minutes.
5. Check if the fish is cooked (if flaky with a fork) and add whiskey, soy sauce, and oregano to taste.
6. Adjust the seasoning, garnish with parsley, and it's ready to serve.

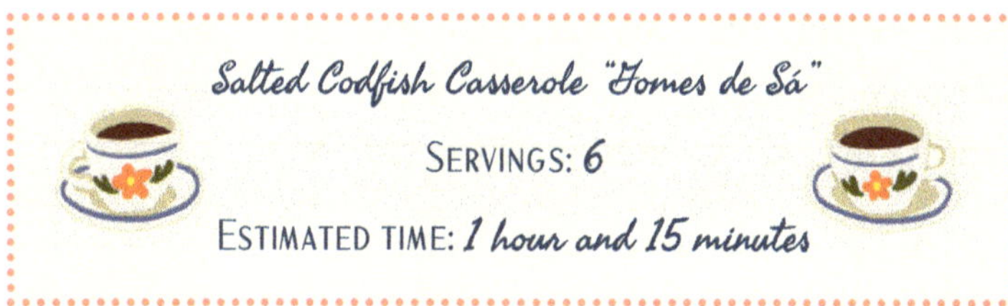

Salted Codfish Casserole "Gomes de Sá"

SERVINGS: *6*

ESTIMATED TIME: *1 hour and 15 minutes*

Ingredients

- 2 cod fillets
- 4 large potatoes, halved, skin on
- 1 ½ tbsp olive oil
- 2 large onions, cut in rounds
- 1 clove garlic, minced
- 8 oz cooked garbanzo beans
- Salt and pepper
- 4 eggs, boiled and sliced in rounds
- Black olives
- 1 sprig parsley

Preparation

1. Preheat oven to 390°F.
2. Boil water in a pan and add the cod. Boil for 7 minutes.
3. Remove from the water and remove the skin and bones, then shred.
4. Boil water in a separate pan and salt. Boil potatoes for 10 to 20 minutes, until fork tender.
5. Drain the water and let the potatoes cool slightly. Remove the skin and cut into rounds.
6. Sauté onions and garlic with olive oil in a pan, until lightly browned.
7. In a baking dish, add the cod pieces, garbanzo beans, potato rounds, salt, and pepper. Mix carefully so as not to break in pieces or become mushy.
8. Bake for 15 minutes.

9. Remove from the oven and top with boiled eggs, olives, and chopped parsley.
10. Serve the Cod á Gomes de Sá immediately.

Sautéed Rice with Vegetables

Servings: *4*

Estimated time: *30 minutes*

Ingredients

- Olive oil
- ½ red bell pepper, cut into long, thin strips
- ½ green bell pepper, cut into long, thin strips
- ½ yellow bell pepper, cut into long, thin strips
- ½ zucchini, diced
- ½ onion, diced
- 1 carrot, cut into long, thin strips
- 1 head broccoli, cut into small pieces
- 3 white mushrooms, sliced
- 1 ½ cup of cooked white rice
- Tamari (gluten-free soy sauce)
- 6 cherry tomatoes, cut into halves
- Handful of chopped parsley

Preparation

1. Add a drizzle of olive oil to the wok and heat on high.
2. Add all the vegetables to the wok and sauté for at least 5 minutes.
3. Then add the cooked rice and let it fry a little.
4. To finish, add tamari to taste and sauté while continuing to stir.
5. Serve with chopped parsley and cherry tomatoes

Sweet and Sour Chicken

SERVINGS: 4-6

ESTIMATED TIME: 40 minutes

Ingredients

- 3 tsp sunflower oil
- 4 chicken breasts, diced
- Salt and pepper
- ¼ cup 1 tbsp grated ginger
- 1 red bell pepper, diced
- 1 green bell pepper, diced
- 2 onions, chopped
- 8 oz can cut pineapple in syrup
- 4 tbsp vinegar
- 1 tsp cornstarch
- Soy sauce (or tamari)

Preparation

1. Season the chicken pieces with salt, pepper, and ginger.
2. In a large frying pan, heat the oil over high heat and pan fry the chicken until golden.
3. Add both peppers and onions and fry well.
4. Add the pineapple pieces (save the syrup) and mix them with the chicken. Continue frying.
5. In a separate bowl, mix half of the pineapple syrup with the vinegar, cornstarch, and soy sauce, to taste.
6. Add the syrup mixture to the sautéed chicken and bring to a boil.
7. Reduce the heat and stir until thickened.
8. Serve immediately with rice.

Desserts

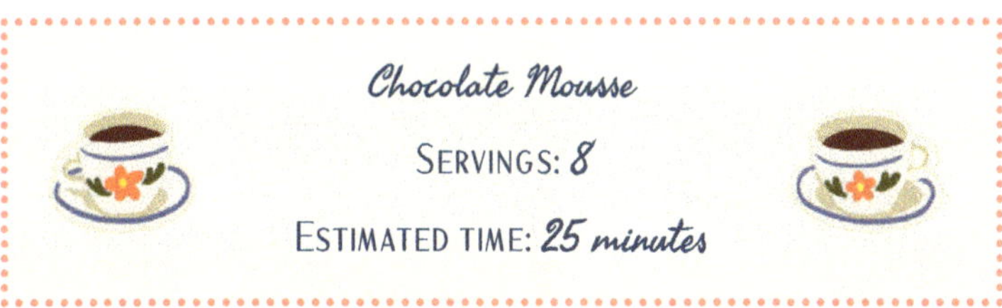

Ingredients

- 8 oz culinary chocolate
- 6 eggs, separated
- 1 tbsp white sugar
- ¼ cup salted margarine

Preparation

1. Melt the chocolate with margarine in a bain-marie, over medium heat until the chocolate melts. Remove from heat.
2. Beat the egg whites until stiff.
3. Add a spoonful of sugar to the egg yolks and mix with a hand mixer until well beaten.
4. Add the chocolate to the beaten egg whites and mix with a wire whisk.
5. Combine chocolate mixture with egg yolk mixture. Stir carefully by hand.
6. Place equal amounts in individual decorative bowls and refrigerate until served.

Almond Tart

SERVINGS: 8

ESTIMATED TIME: 40 minutes

Ingredients

Dough

- ½ cup white sugar
- 3 eggs
- ¾ cup flour
- ½ cup margarine, melted and slightly cooled
- 1 tsp baking powder

Cream

- ⅔ cup sliced almonds
- ½ cup white sugar
- ½ cup margarine
- Scant ½ cup milk

Preparation

1. Preheat the oven to 350°F.
2. Mix the sugar with the eggs, then add the flour, baking powder, and margarine until combined.
3. Grease the pan with margarine, sprinkle with flour, and add the dough.
4. Bake for 20 minutes.
5. Add all the cream ingredients to a pan and heat on high until caramelized.
6. Pour over the baked tart and return to the oven until the cream turns golden.
7. Ready to serve.

Grandma's Candy

SERVINGS: *8-10*

ESTIMATED TIME: *20 minutes to prepare; 1 hour to chill*

Ingredients

- 8 oz condensed milk
- 8 oz regular whole milk
- 4 eggs, separated
- 1 tbsp instant coffee
- Tea biscuits
- ¼ cup white sugar
- 1 cup heavy cream

Preparation

1. Cook the condensed and regular milk with the egg yolks in a pan, stirring continuously until thickened.
2. Prepare the coffee with a little cold water. Then soak the biscuits in the coffee.
3. On a tray, fill the bottom with the coffee-soaked biscuits.
4. Remove the milk mixture from the stove and pour it over the biscuits.
5. In a bowl, beat the egg whites and sugar with a hand mixer until stiff.
6. Whip the heavy cream and mix it with the egg whites.
7. Place it on top of the biscuits and refrigerate for 1 hour.
8. Decorate with biscuits broken into pieces or crushed, depending on your taste

Apple Pie

SERVINGS: *8*

ESTIMATED TIME: *40 minutes*

Ingredients

- 2 eggs
- ½ cup + 2 tbsp white sugar
- ½ cup + 2 tbsp flour
- 6 tbsp whole milk
- 5 tbsp oil
- 1 pinch salt
- Unsalted butter
- Apples with skin on, thinly sliced
- Cinnamon, as desired

Preparation

1. Preheat the oven to 350°F. Grease a pie pan with butter and sprinkle with flour.
2. Add eggs, sugar, flour, milk, oil, and salt in a bowl and beat very well.
3. Place the mixture in the greased pie pan.
4. Place overlapping apple slices on top, circling the pan until mixture is completely covered.
5. Dust with cinnamon and place in the oven for 20 minutes.

www.ingramcontent.com/pod-product-compliance
Ingram Content Group UK Ltd.
Pitfield, Milton Keynes, MK11 3LW, UK
UKHW021918270726
14059UKWH00002B/86

9 781945 783548